Name

K

Zaner-Bloser

Handwriting

Zaner-Bloser
A Highlights Company

Dear Family,

Welcome to *Zaner-Bloser Handwriting*! Throughout your child's handwriting book, you'll see Digital Tutor QR codes. Help your child scan the codes with a mobile device to access instructional videos that reinforce the basics of handwriting and how to write letters and numerals. Turn to page 1 for more information.

Occupational Therapy Consultants
Asha Asher, MA OTR/L, FAOTA, MEd (Special Education), Redlands, CA
Carol Armann, OTR/L, Marietta, OH

ELL Consultants
Ellen Riojas Clark, PhD, Professor Emerita of Bicultural-Bilingual Studies, University of Texas at San Antonio
Patricia Sánchez, PhD, Professor of Bicultural-Bilingual Studies, University of Texas at San Antonio

Reviewers
Julia Ann Agard, University of Nebraska at Kearney, NE
Jeffrey Armann, Frontier Local School District, OH
Ramona Blair, Bellwood School District 88, IL
Denise Brosius, Caesar Rodney School District, DE
Dr. James Troutman, Ed.D., University of Houston, TX
Kathy Twaroski, Ashwaubenon School District, WI
Valerie White, St. Anne's Episcopal School, Middletown, DE
Iefay A. Williams, School District of Philadelphia, PA

ISBN 978-1-4531-1927-3

This book is printed on paper certified by third-party standards for sustainably managed forestry.

Zaner-Bloser, Inc.
800.421.3018
zaner-bloser.com
Printed in the United States of America

14 2023

ZB Code 20

Table of Contents

Unit 1: Getting Started

Unit 2: Writing Letters

Unit 3: Writing Numerals

Unit 4: Using What You Have Learned

Explore Your Book

Meet Zaney

Zaney will be popping up in your book to help you form letters and make sure your writing is easy to read!

Digital Tutor

Scan the **Digital Tutor** codes with a mobile device to watch Zaney's videos. You will learn how to write your best letters!

Digital Tutor
Introduction

Models and Guidelines

Arrows show how to write letters.

Start at the green dot.

Colored lines help you write.

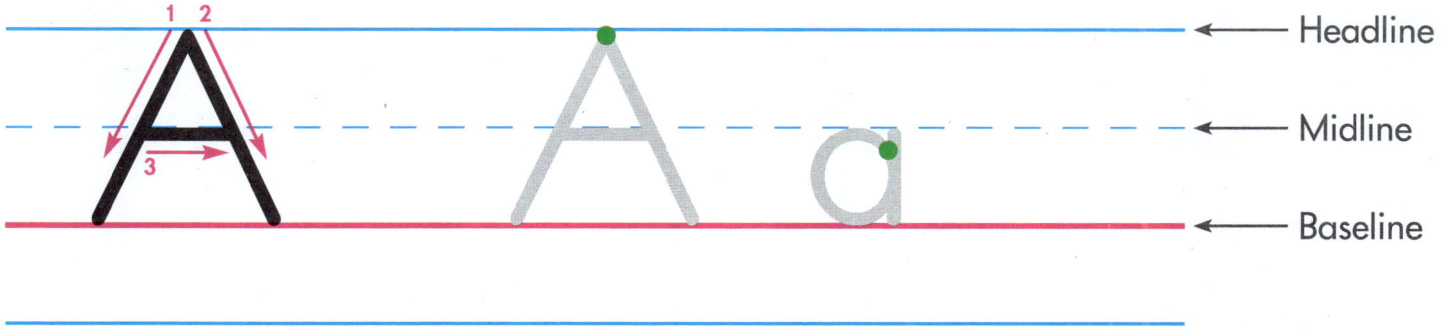

Digital Tutor
Writing on the Lines

Stop and Check

Stop and circle the best letter you wrote.

Digital Tutor
Stop and Check

Pretest

Draw a picture.

Draw shapes you know.

Write letters you know.

Discover

Left and Right

Trace your **left** hand on this mitten.

Trace your **right** hand on this mitten.

Writing Positions

Left-Handed Writers If you use your left hand to write, follow the rules on this page.

Sit up tall.
Keep your feet on the floor.

Digital Tutor
Sitting Position

Digital Tutor
Paper Position

Slant your paper.

Put both arms on the desk.

Pull your pencil toward your left elbow.

Use your right hand to move the paper.

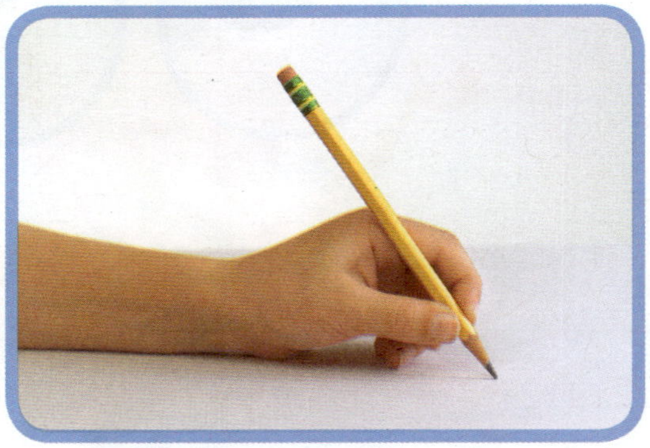

Digital Tutor
Pencil Position

Hold the pencil like this.

Do not squeeze the pencil when you write.

Right-Handed Writers If you use your right hand to write, follow the rules on this page.

Sit up tall.

Keep both feet on the floor.

Digital Tutor

Sitting Position

Digital Tutor

Paper Position

Keep your paper straight.

Put both arms on the desk.

Pull your pencil toward the middle of your body.

Use your left hand to move the paper.

Digital Tutor

Pencil Position

Hold the pencil like this.

Do not squeeze the pencil when you write.

Write

Basic Strokes

Vertical Lines You use vertical lines when you write.
Look at the vertical strokes below.
Trace them with your finger.

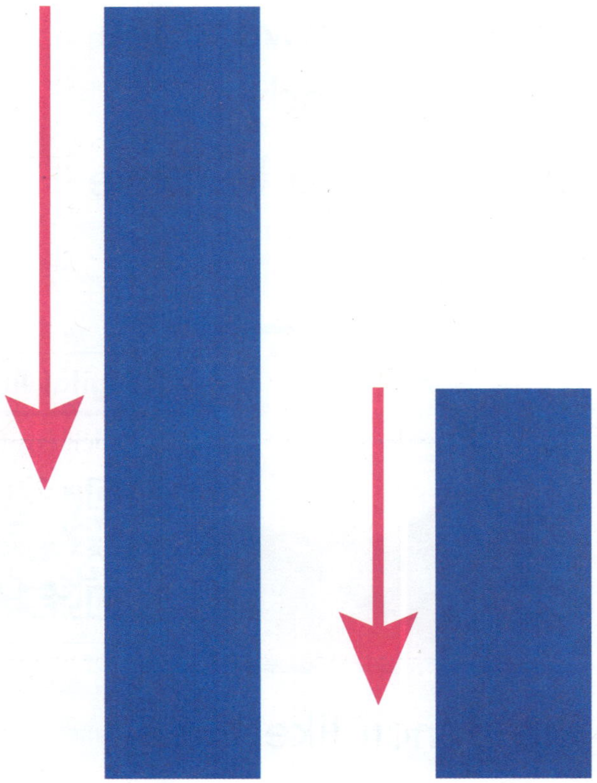

Find vertical lines in the picture above.
Draw this picture or one of your own.

Use your finger to trace the vertical lines in the letters and numerals.

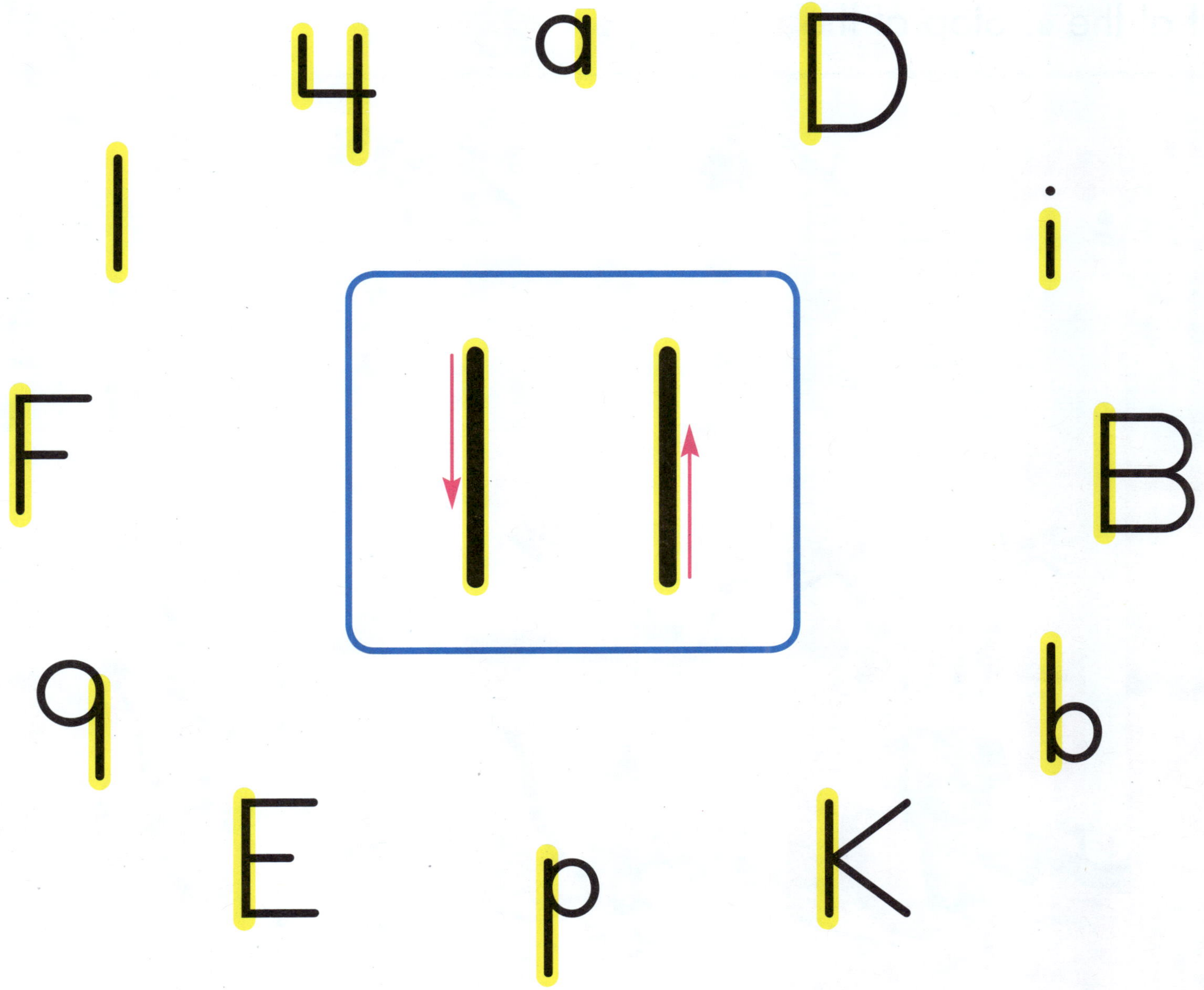

Write

Basic Strokes

Vertical Lines Write vertical lines.
Start at the ●. Stop at the ●.

Write vertical lines.
Start at the ●. Stop at the ●.

Trace the lines.

Write

Basic Strokes

Horizontal Lines You use horizontal lines when you write. Look at the horizontal lines below. Trace them with your finger.

Find horizontal lines in the picture above. Draw this picture or one of your own.

Use your finger to trace the horizontal lines in the letters and numerals.

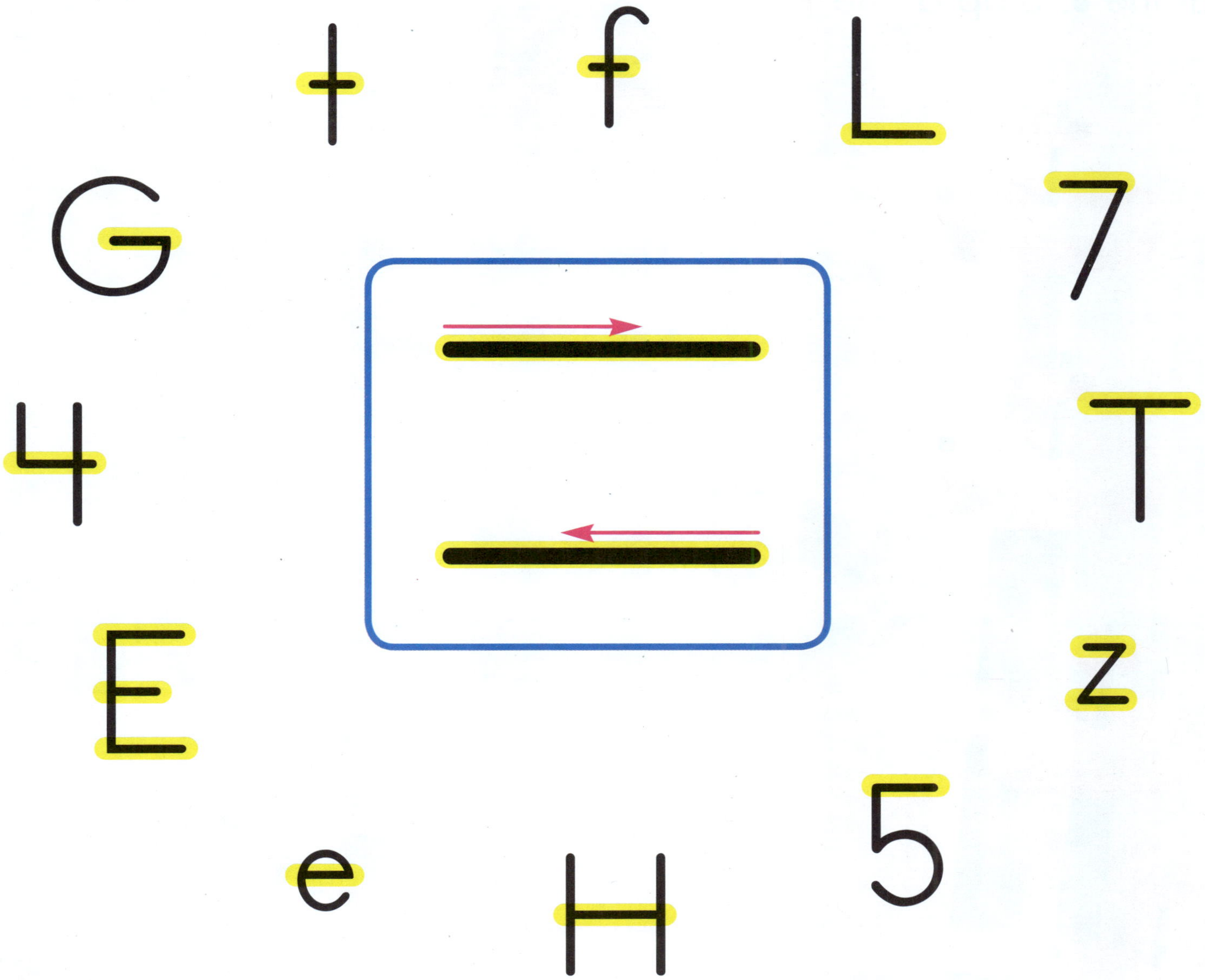

Write

Basic Strokes

Horizontal Lines Write horizontal lines.
Start at the ●. Stop at the ●.

Write horizontal lines.
Start at the ●. Stop at the ●.

Trace the lines.

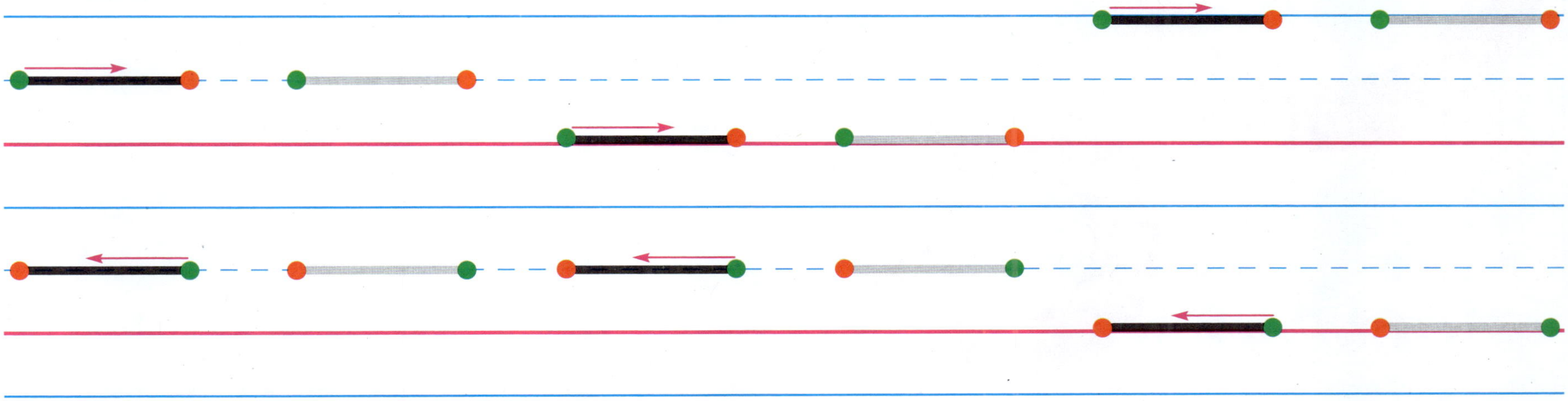

Basic Strokes

Backward Circle Lines You use backward circle lines when you write. Look at the circle lines below. Trace them with your finger.

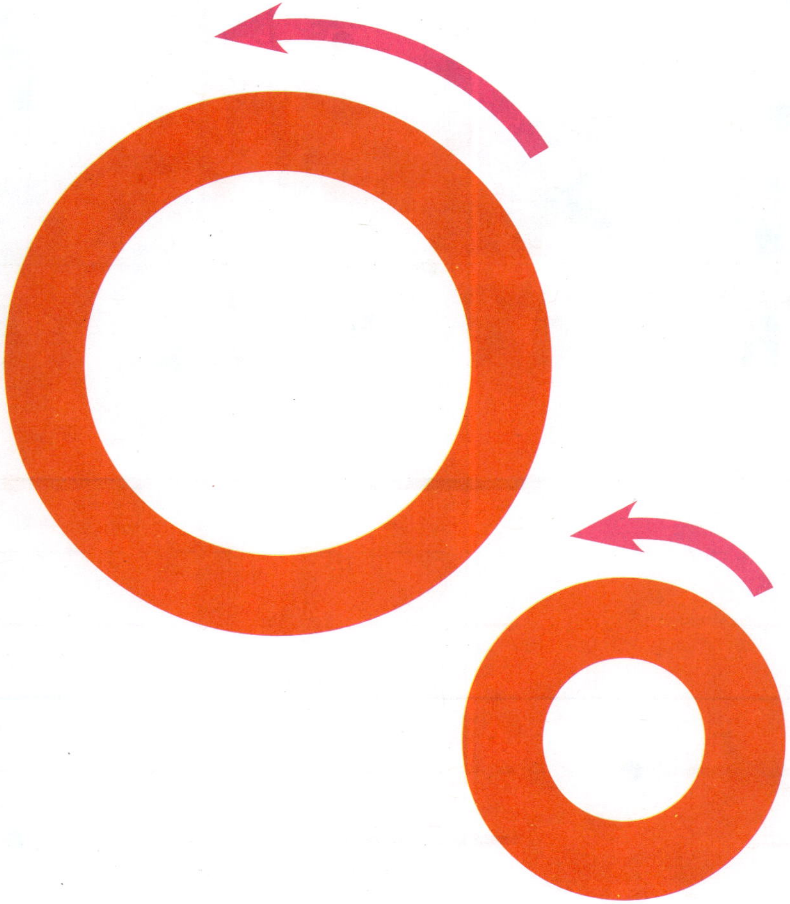

Find circle lines in the picture above. Draw this picture or one of your own.

Use your finger to trace the backward circle lines in the letters and numerals.

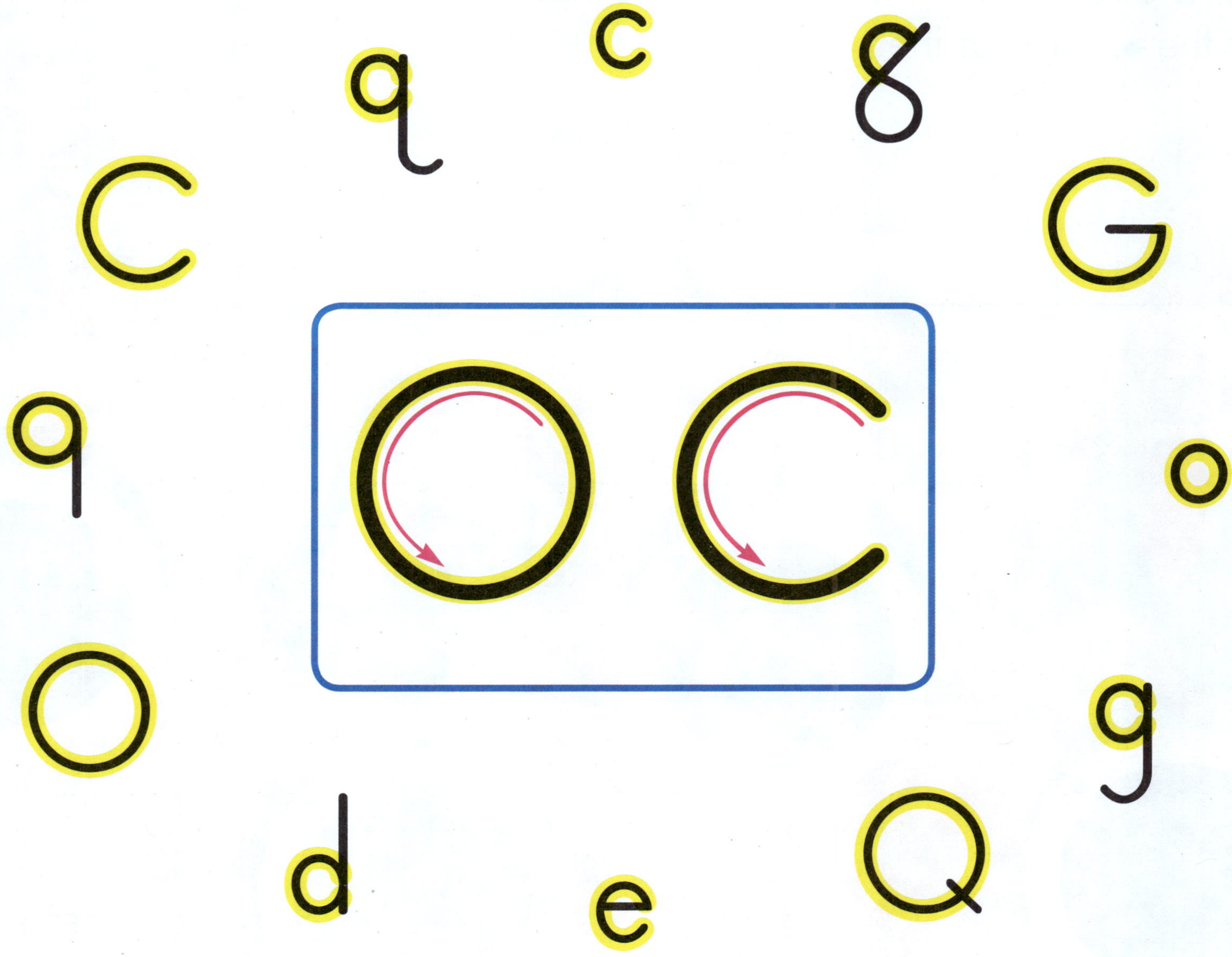

Write

Basic Strokes

Backward Circle Lines Write backward circle lines.
Start at the ●. Stop at the ●.

Write backward circle lines.
Start at the ●. Stop at the ●.

Trace the lines.

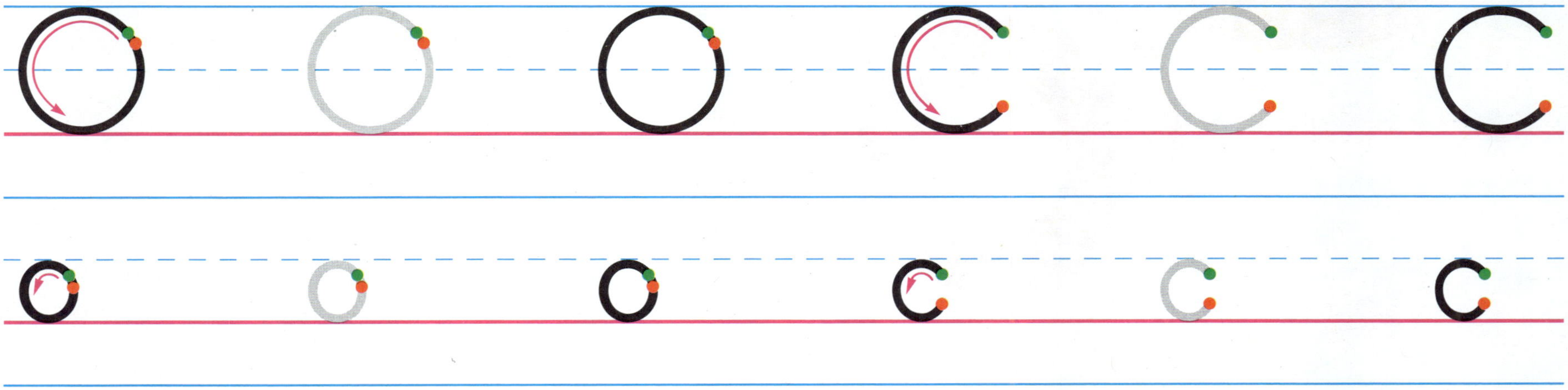

Write

Basic Strokes

Forward Circle Lines You use forward circle lines when you write. Look at the circle lines below. Trace them with your finger.

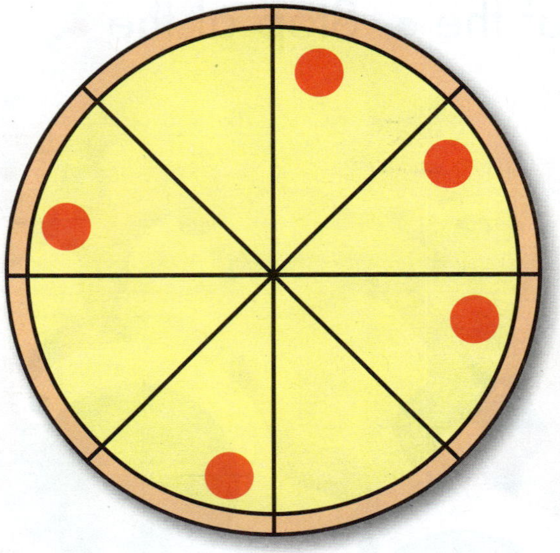

Find circle lines in the picture above. Draw this picture or one of your own.

Use your finger to trace the forward circle lines in the letters and numerals.

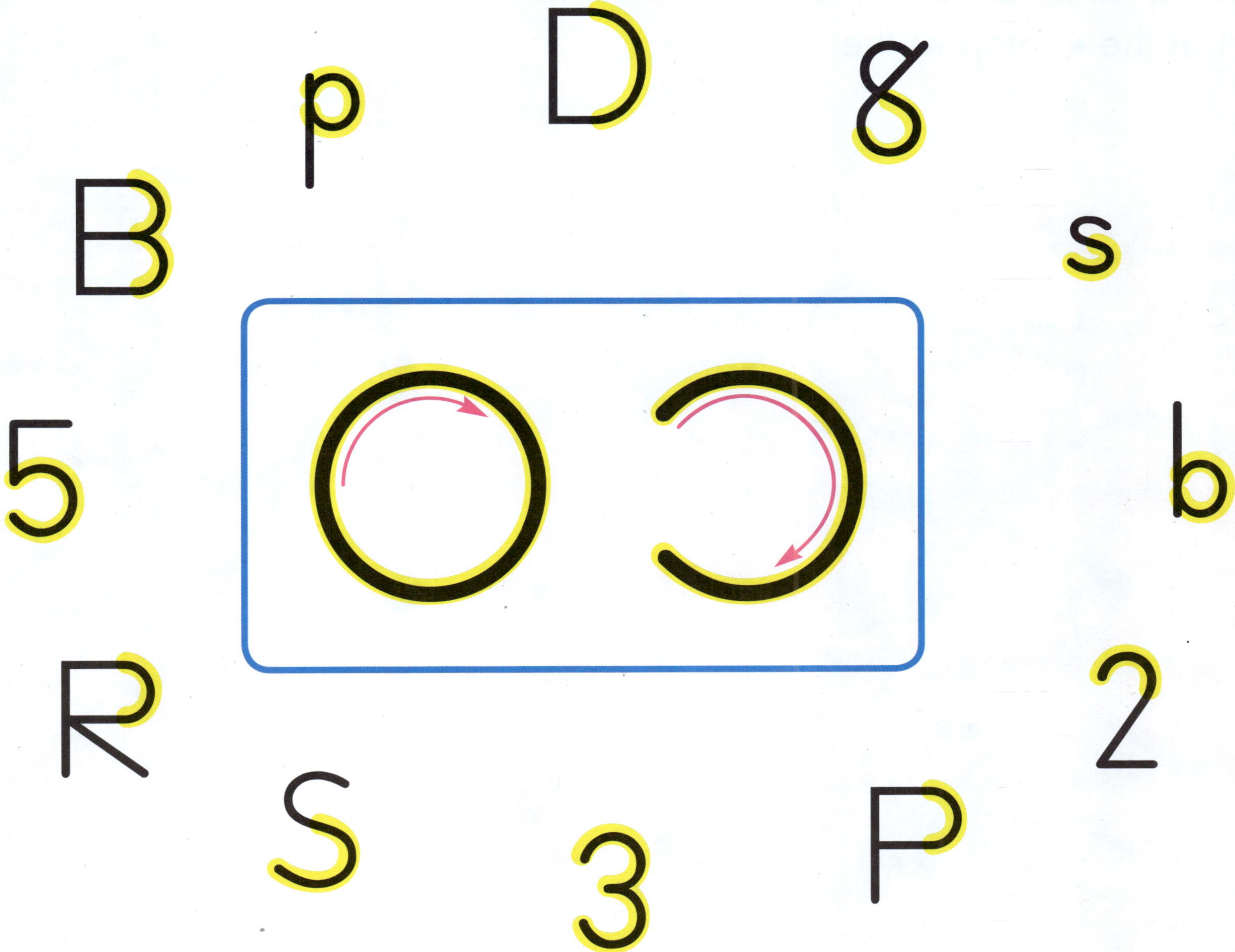

Write

Basic Strokes

Forward Circle Lines Write forward circle lines.
Start at the ●. Stop at the ●.

Write forward circle lines.
Start at the ●. Stop at the ●.

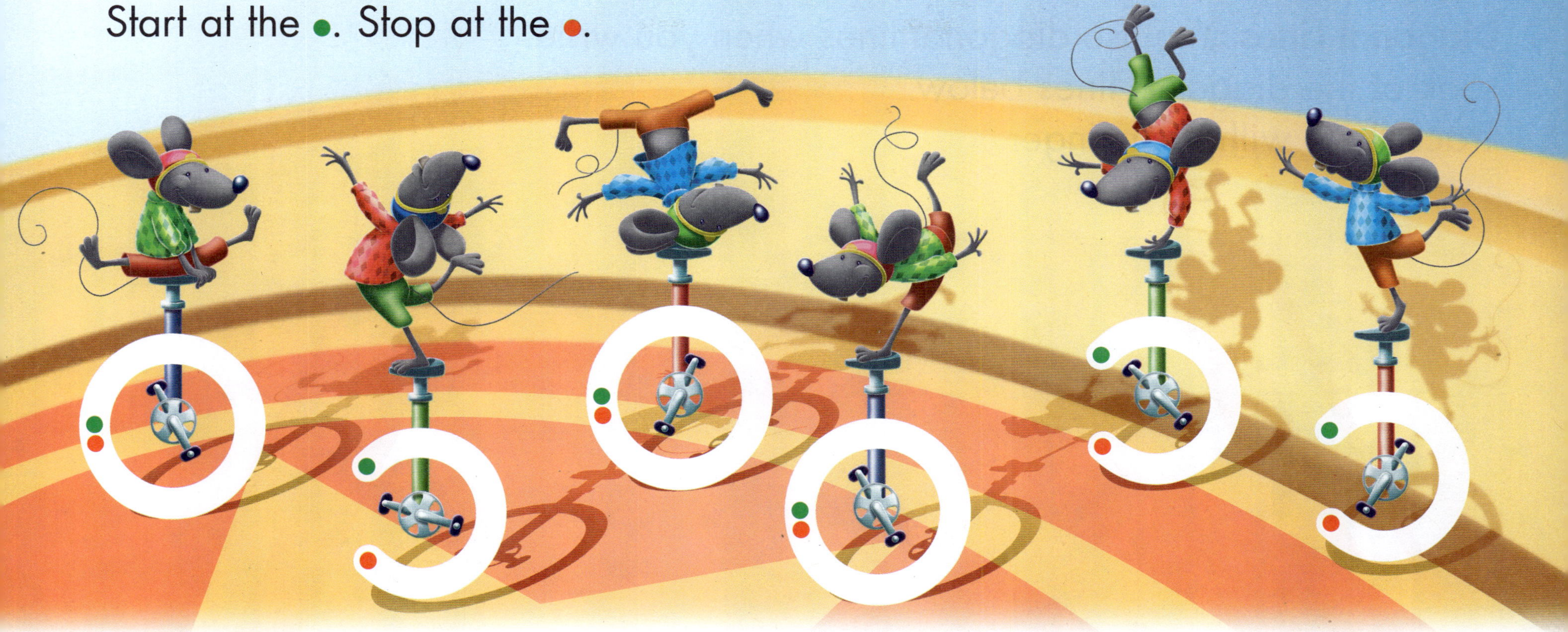

Trace the lines.

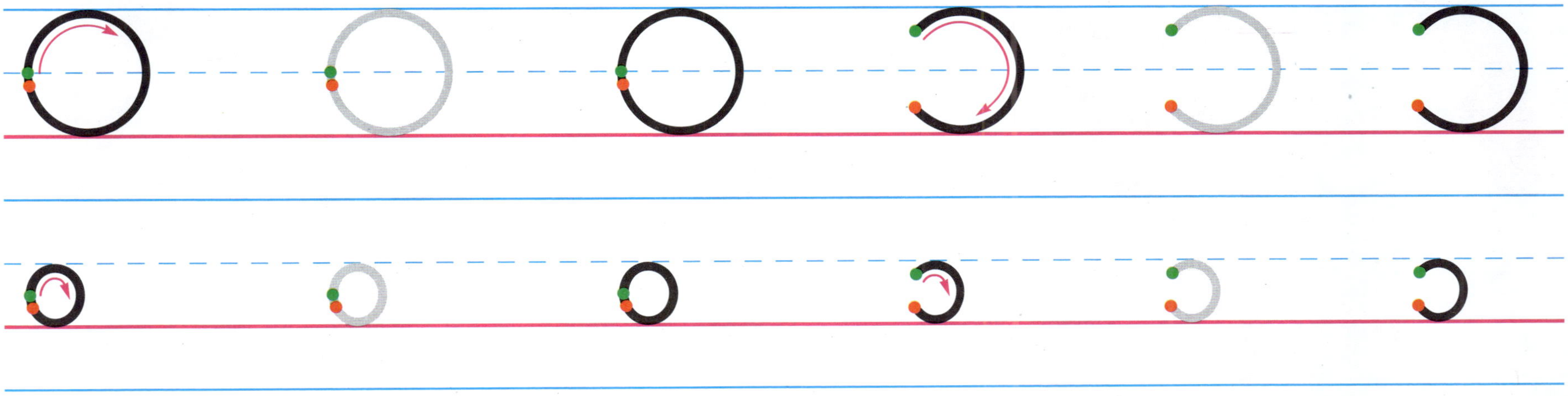

Write

Basic Strokes

Diagonal Lines You use diagonal lines when you write.
Look at the diagonal lines below.
Trace them with your finger.

Look at the diagonal lines below.
Trace them with your finger.

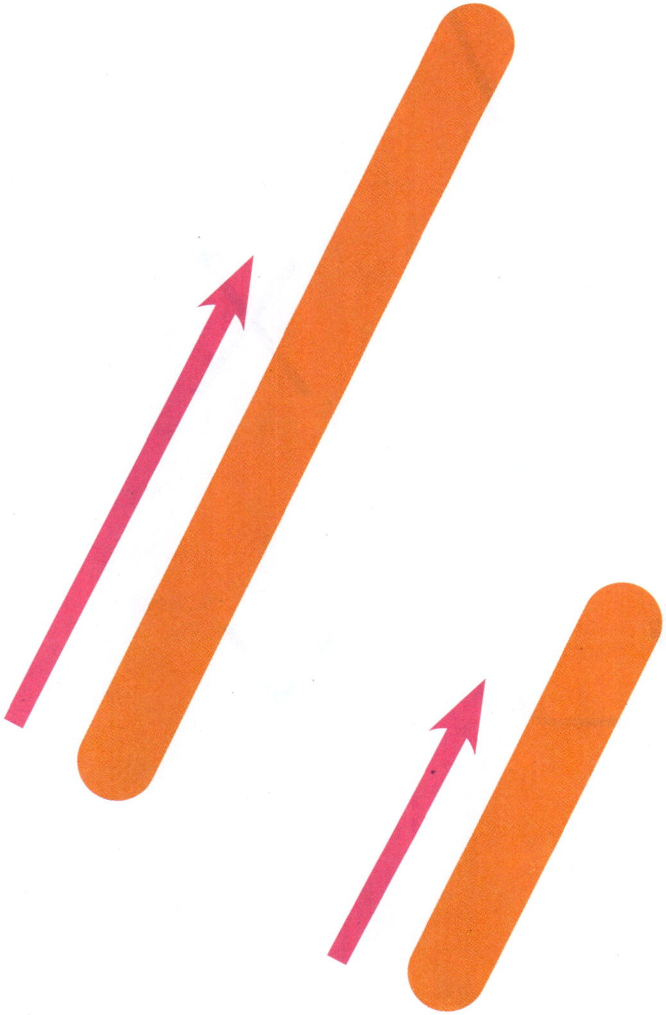

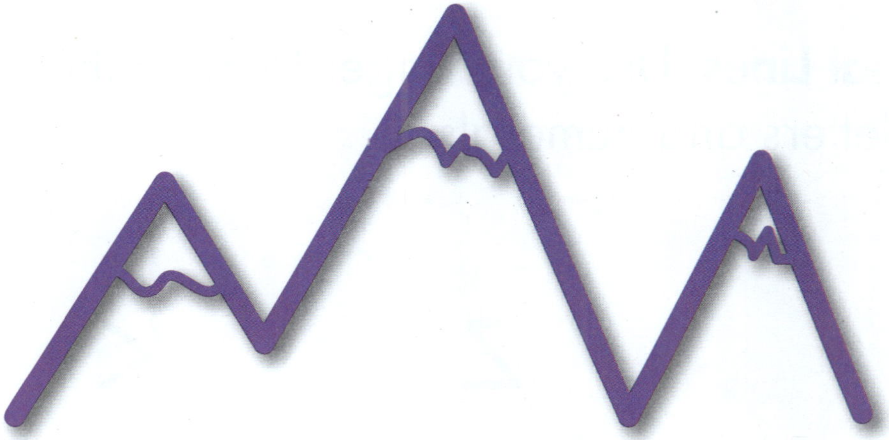

Find diagonal lines in the picture above.
Draw this picture or one of your own.

Basic Strokes

Diagonal Lines Use your finger to trace the diagonal lines in the letters and numerals.

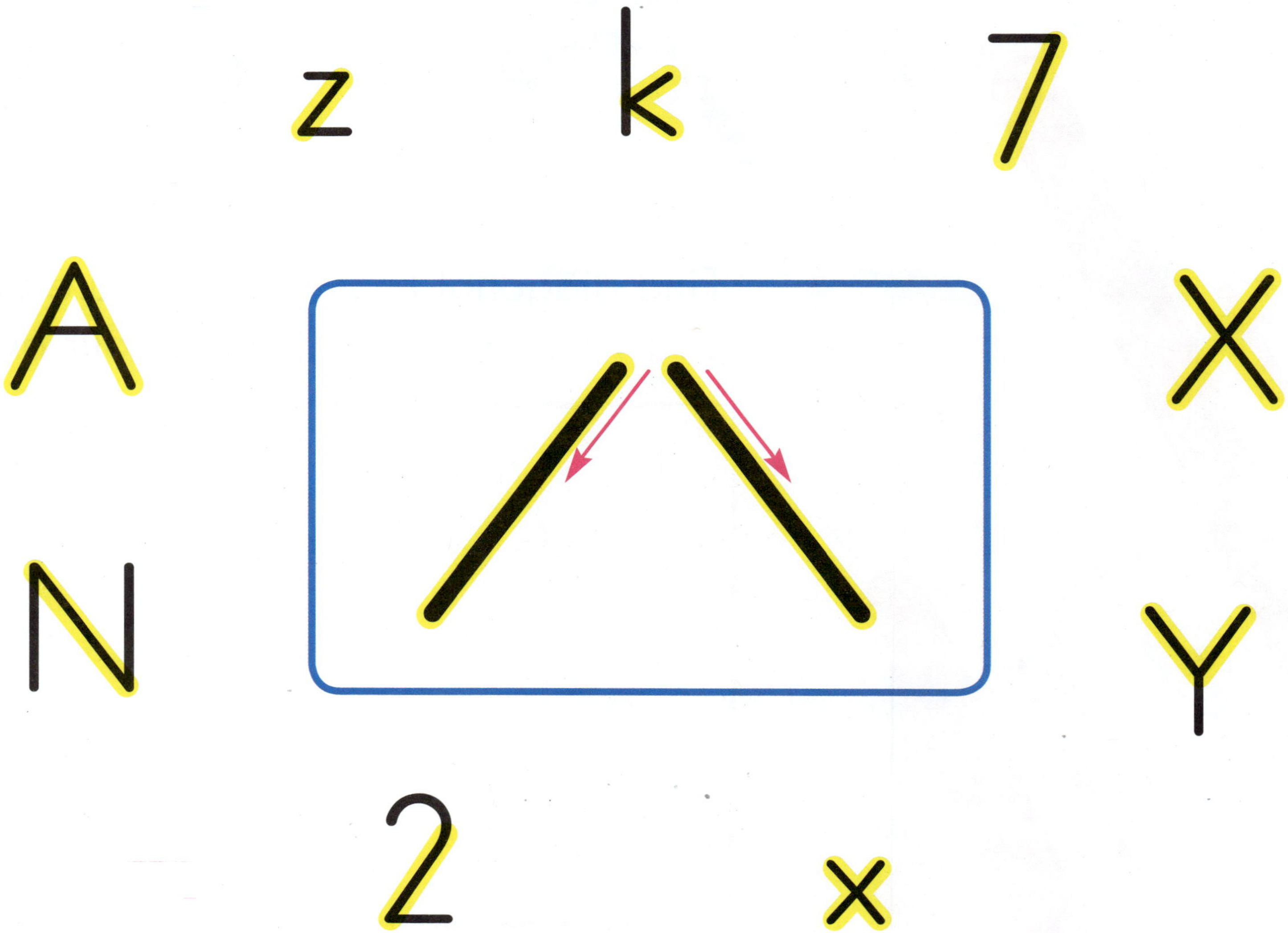

M w

V v

W

Write

Basic Strokes

Diagonal Lines Write diagonal lines.
Start at the ●. Stop at the ●.

Write diagonal lines.
Start at the ●. Stop at the ●.

Trace the lines.

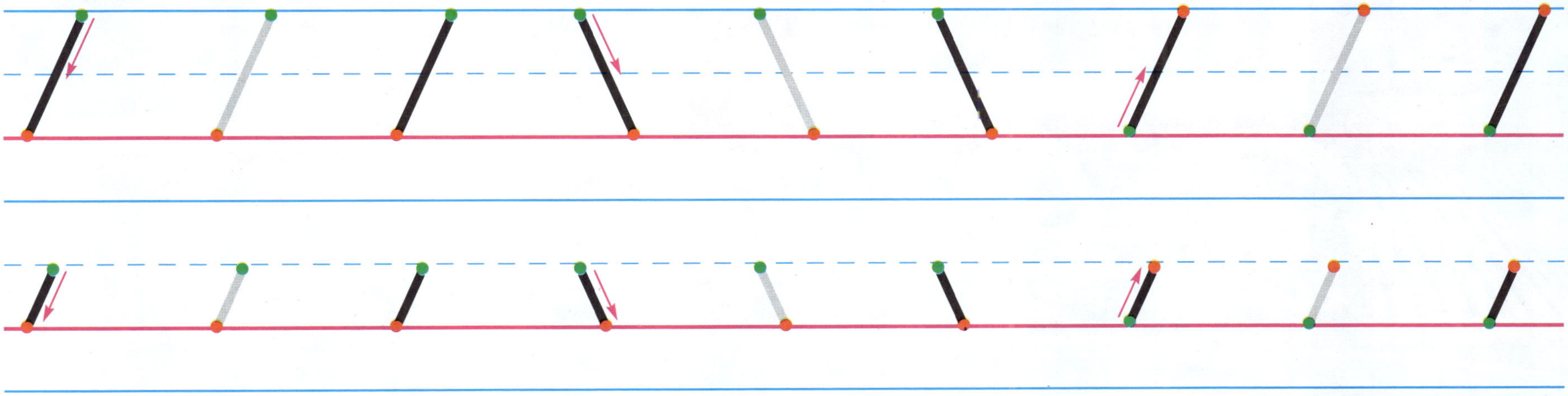

Review

Basic Strokes

Digital Tutor
Basic Strokes

Name the shape of each window. Use the basic strokes to draw a line around each one.

Use the basic strokes to draw a line around each window.

Write

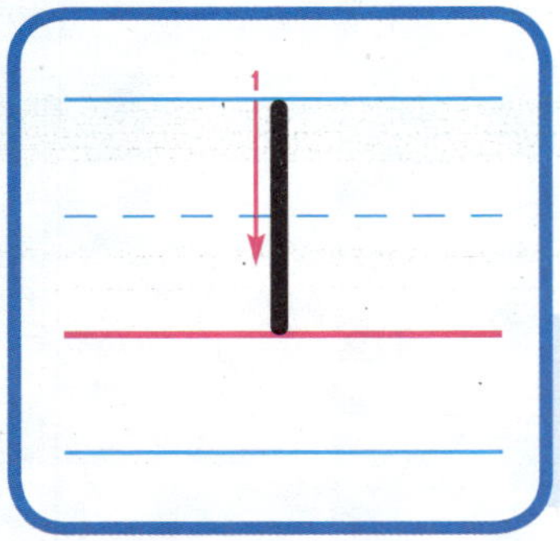

Trace and write. ✔ Circle your best **l**.

l l l l l l l

lion leaf lemon

Digital Tutor
Letter Model and Formation

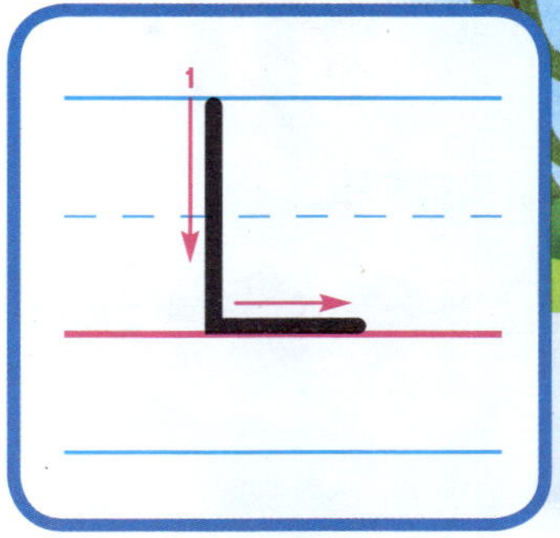

1. Pull down straight. Slide right.

Trace and write. Circle your best **L**.

L L L L L L L

Lemonade Leo Lisa

Digital Tutor
Letter Model and Formation

Write

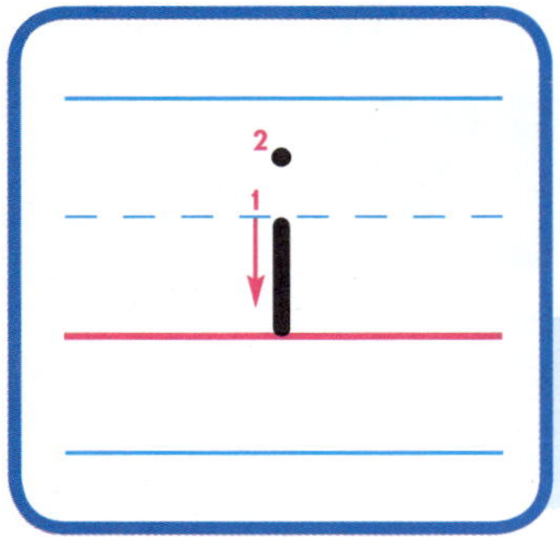

1. Pull down straight. Lift.
2. Dot.

Trace and write. ✔ Circle your best **i**.

i i i i i i i

inchworm itch insect

Digital Tutor

Letter Model and Formation

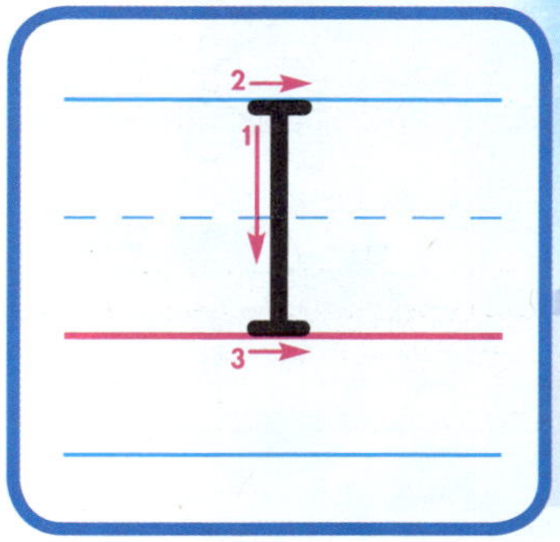

1. Pull down straight. Lift.
2. Slide right. Lift.
3. Slide right.

Trace and write. Circle your best **I**.

I I I I I I I

Insect Island Ian

Digital Tutor

Letter Model and Formation

Write

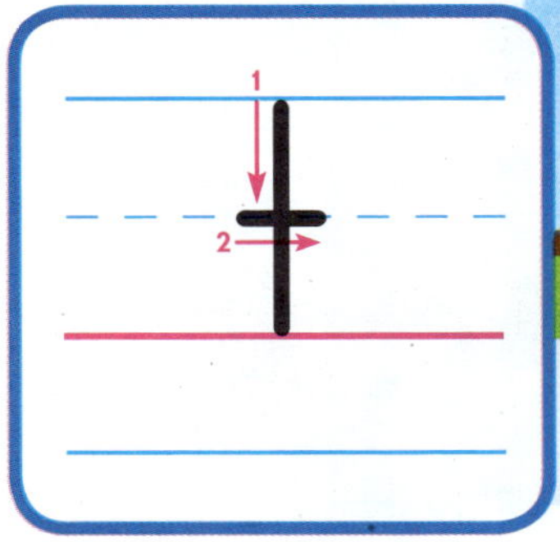

1. Pull down straight. Lift.
2. Slide right.

Trace and write. ✔ Circle your best **t**.

t t t t t t t

train tower track

Digital Tutor

Letter Model and Formation

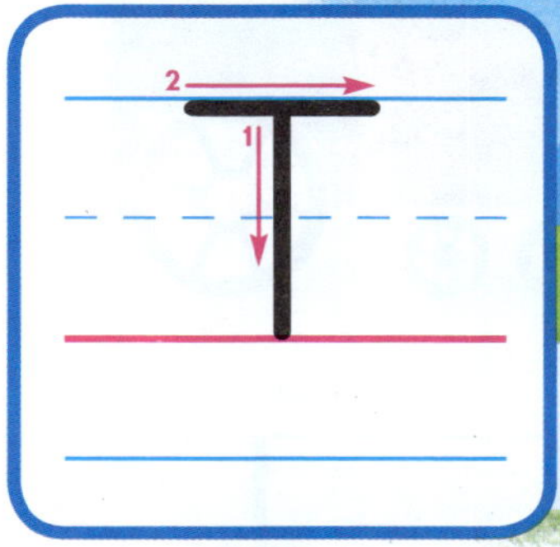

1. Pull down straight. Lift.
2. Slide right.

Trace and write. Circle your best **T**.

T T T T T T T

Toot Tiny Town

Digital Tutor
Letter Model and Formation

Review

Write the letters.

l l

i i

t t

L L

I I

T T

Uppercase Letters Write the missing uppercase letters.

A B C D E

F G H ___ J

K ___ M N O

P Q R S ___

U V W X Y Z

Write

1. Circle back all the way around.

Trace and write. Circle your best **o**.

o

owl open octopus

Digital Tutor
Letter Model and Formation

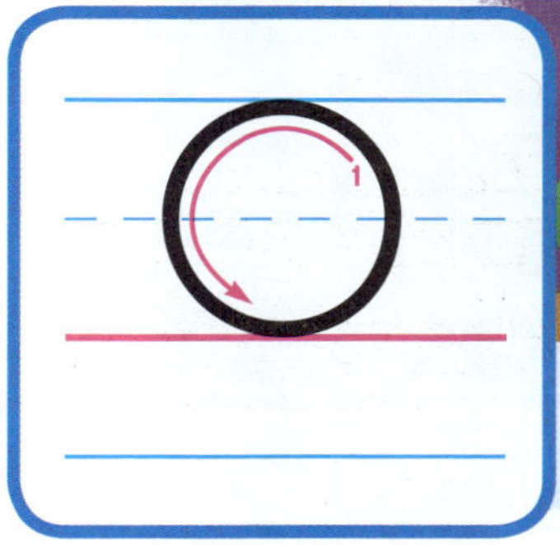

1. Circle back all the way around.

Trace and write. Circle your best O.

O O O O O O O

On Off Olivia

Digital Tutor
Letter Model and Formation

Write

a

1. Circle back all the way around; push up straight. Pull down straight.

Trace and write. Circle your best **a**.

a a a a a a a

apple ants alligator

Digital Tutor

Letter Model and Formation

1. Slant left. Lift.
2. Slant right. Lift.
3. Slide right.

Trace and write. ✓ Circle your best **A**.

A A A A A A A

Avenue Alex Abby

Digital Tutor

Letter Model and Formation

Write

d

1. Circle back all the way around; push up straight. Pull down straight.

Trace and write. Circle your best **d**.

d d d d d d d

dog duck door

Digital Tutor

Letter Model and Formation

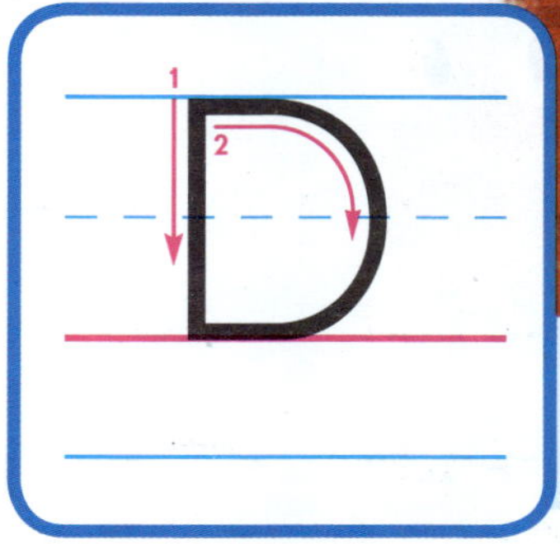

1. Pull down straight. Lift.
2. Slide right; curve forward; slide left.

Trace and write. Circle your best **D**.

D D D D D D D

Don't David Dana

Digital Tutor

Letter Model and Formation

Review

Write the letters.

o o a a d d

O O A A D D

Lowercase Letters Write the missing lowercase letters.

___ b c ___ e

f g h ___ j

k ___ m n ___

p q r s ___

u v w x y z

Write

c

1. Circle back.

Trace and write. Circle your best **c**.

c c c c c c c

cook cake cup

Digital Tutor

Letter Model and Formation

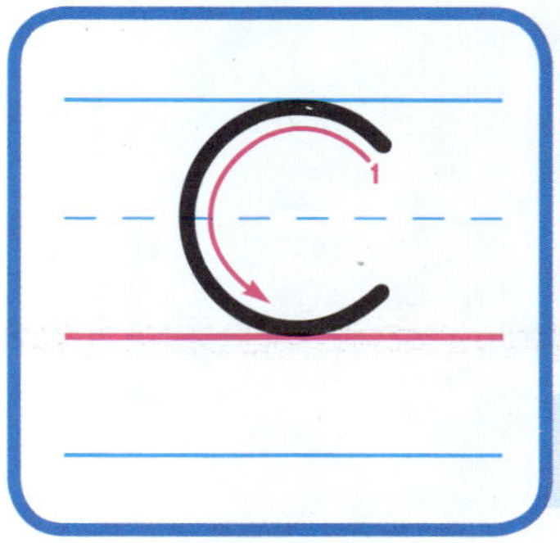

1. Circle back.

Trace and write. ✔ Circle your best **C**.

C C C C C C C

Cakes Cody Camel

Digital Tutor

Letter Model and Formation

Write

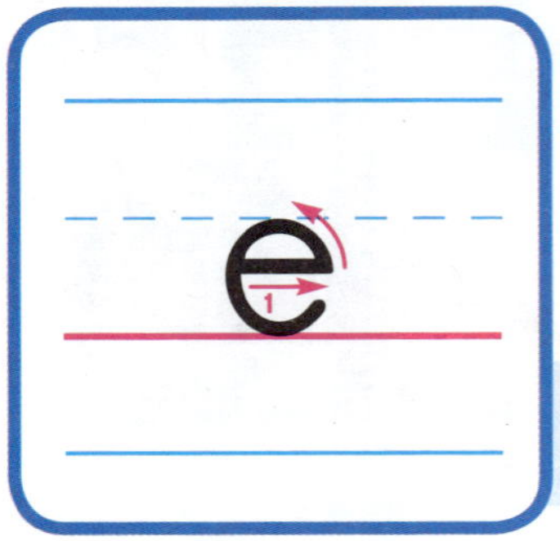

1. Slide right.
   Circle back.

Trace and write. ✔ Circle your best **e**.

e e e e e e e

✔

elephant elk ear

Digital Tutor

Letter Model and Formation

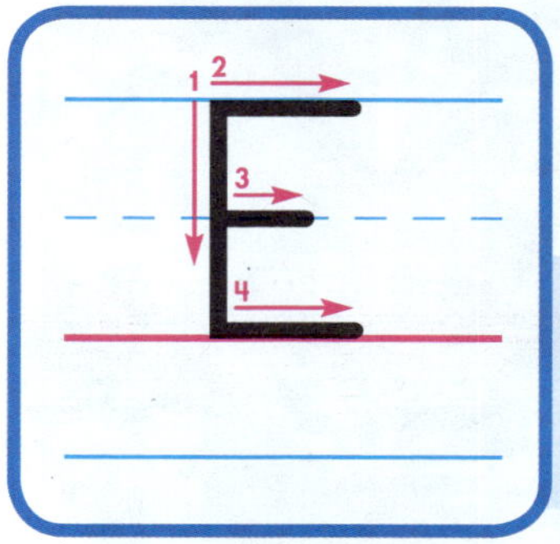

1. Pull down straight. Lift.
2. Slide right. Lift.
3. Slide right; stop short. Lift.
4. Slide right.

Trace and write. Circle your best **E**.

E E E E E E E

Eye Eric Ella

Digital Tutor

Letter Model and Formation

Write

1. Curve back; pull down straight. Lift.
2. Slide right.

Trace and write. ✔ Circle your best **f**.

f f f f f f f

flute fish fly

Digital Tutor
Letter Model and Formation

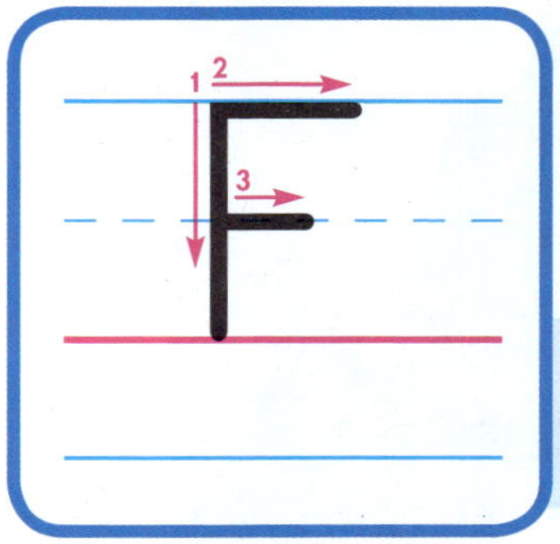

1. Pull down straight. Lift.
2. Slide right. Lift.
3. Slide right; stop short.

Trace and write. Circle your best **F**.

F F F F F F F

Frog Finn Farrah

Digital Tutor

Letter Model and Formation

Review

Write the letters.

c c e e f f

C C E E F F

Uppercase Letters Write the missing uppercase letters.

___ B ___ ___ ___

___ G H ___ J

K ___ M N ___

P Q R S ___

U V W X Y Z

Write

g

1. Circle back all the way around; push up straight. Pull down straight; curve back.

Trace and write. ✔ Circle your best **g**.

g g g g g g g

goat guitar garden

Digital Tutor

Letter Model and Formation

1. Circle back. Slide left.

Trace and write. Circle your best **G**.

G G G G G G G

Good Gwen Gabe

Digital Tutor
Letter Model and Formation

Write

1. Pull down straight; curve back. Lift.
2. Dot.

Trace and write. ✔ Circle your best **j**.

j j j j j j j

jam juice jar

Digital Tutor

Letter Model and Formation

1. Pull down straight; curve back. Lift.
2. Slide right.

Trace and write. ✔ Circle your best **J**.

J J J J J J J

Jack Jill Jay

Digital Tutor
Letter Model and Formation

Write

1. Circle back all the way around; push up straight. Pull down straight; curve forward.

Trace and write. ✔ Circle your best **q**.

q q q q q q q

queen quail quilt

Digital Tutor

Letter Model and Formation

1. Circle back all the way around. Lift.
2. Slant right.

Trace and write. ✔ Circle your best **Q**.

Q Q Q Q Q Q Q

Quiet Quack Quinn

Digital Tutor

Letter Model and Formation

Review

Write the letters.

g g

j j

q q

G G

J J

Q Q

Lowercase Letters Write the missing lowercase letters.

___ b ___ ___ ___

___ ___ h ___ ___

k ___ m n ___

p ___ r s ___

u v w x y z

Write

u

1. Pull down straight; curve forward; push up. Pull down straight.

Trace and write. ✔ Circle your best **u**.

u u u u u u u

umbrella up under

Digital Tutor

Letter Model and Formation

1. Pull down straight; curve forward; push up.

Trace and write. ✔ Circle your best **U**.

U U U U U U U

Upside Uma Uri

Digital Tutor

Letter Model and Formation

Write

Trace and write. Circle your best **s**.

s s s s s s s

sun slide swing

Digital Tutor
Letter Model and Formation

S

1. Curve back;
curve forward.

Trace and write. ✓ Circle your best **S**.

S S S S S S S

Stop School Street

Digital Tutor

Letter Model and Formation

Write

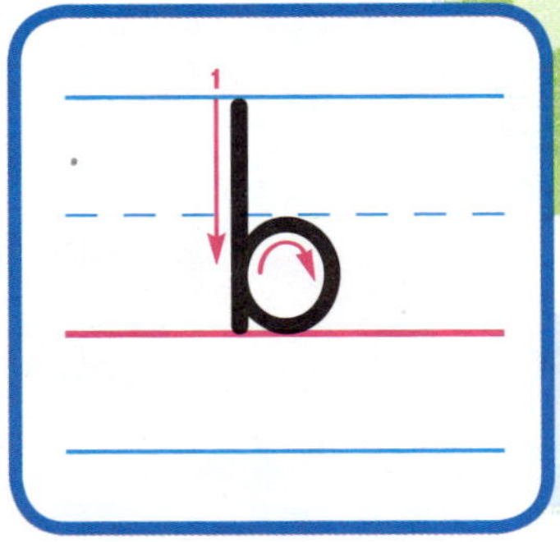

1. Pull down straight.
Push up; circle forward.

Trace and write. ✓ Circle your best **b**.

b b b b b b b

bear balloon bird

Digital Tutor

Letter Model and Formation

B

1. Pull down straight. Lift.
2. Slide right; curve forward; slide left.
Slide right; curve forward; slide left.

Trace and write. Circle your best **B**.

B B B B B B B

Baby Bear Ben

Digital Tutor
Letter Model and Formation

Write

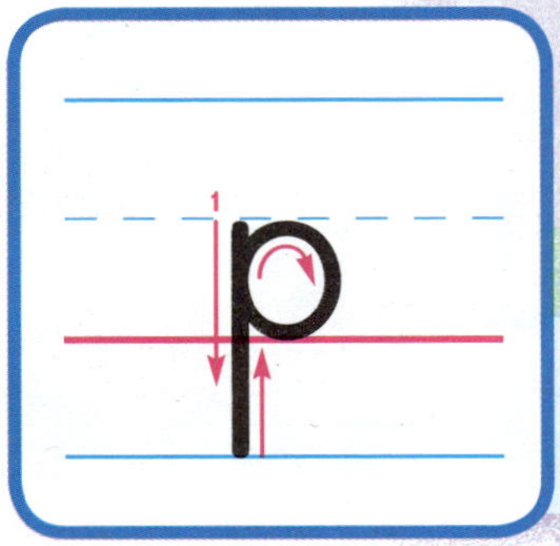

1. Pull down straight.
Push up; circle forward.

Trace and write. Circle your best **p**.

p p p p p p p

pig parrot poodle

Digital Tutor
Letter Model and Formation

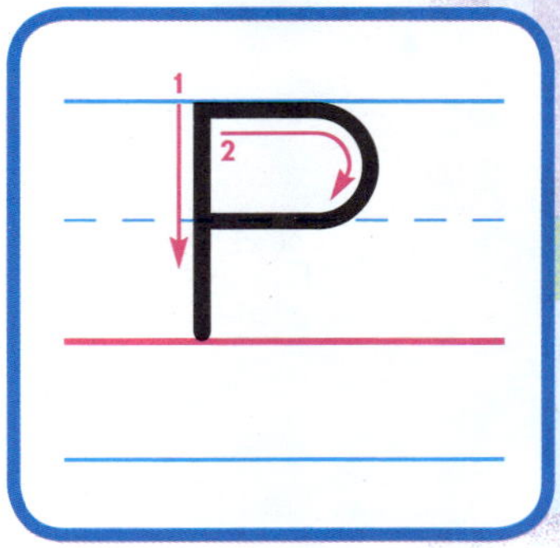

1. Pull down straight. Lift.
2. Slide right; curve forward; slide left.

Trace and write. ✓ Circle your best **P**.

P P P P P P P

Pet Pam Peter

Digital Tutor

Letter Model and Formation

Review

Write the letters.

u u s s b b p p

U U S S B B P P

Apply

Uppercase Letters Write the missing uppercase letters.

H

K M N

R

V W X Y Z

Write

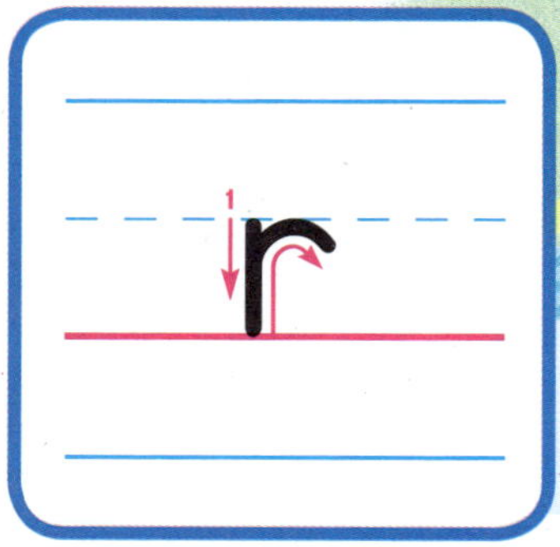

1. Pull down straight. Push up; curve forward.

Trace and write. ✓ Circle your best **r**.

r r r r r r r

rabbit red rowboat

Digital Tutor

Letter Model and Formation

1. Pull down straight. Lift.
2. Slide right; curve forward; slide left. Slant right.

Trace and write. ✓ Circle your best **R**.

R R R R R R R

Rides Rob Rachel

Digital Tutor
Letter Model and Formation

Write

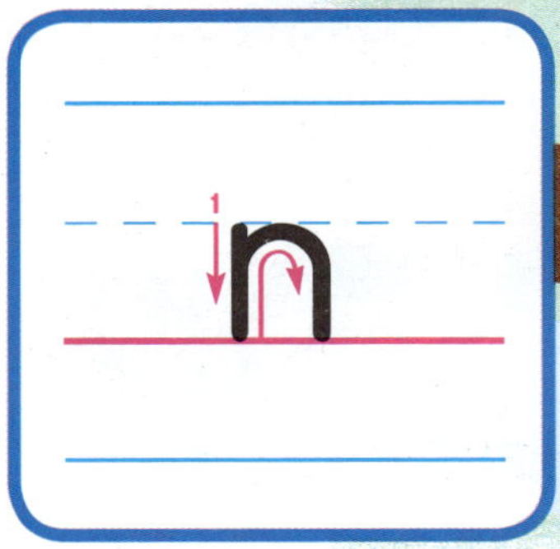

1. Pull down straight.
Push up; curve forward;
pull down straight.

Trace and write. Circle your best **n**.

n n n n n n n

numbers nest nine

Digital Tutor
Letter Model and Formation

1. Pull down straight. Lift.
2. Slant right. Push up straight.

Trace and write. Circle your best **N**.

N N N N N N N

News Nick Natalie

Digital Tutor

Letter Model and Formation

Write

m

1. Pull down straight. Push up; curve forward; pull down straight. Push up; curve forward; pull down straight.

Trace and write. ✔ Circle your best **m**.

m m m m m m m

milk mouse moon

Digital Tutor

Letter Model and Formation

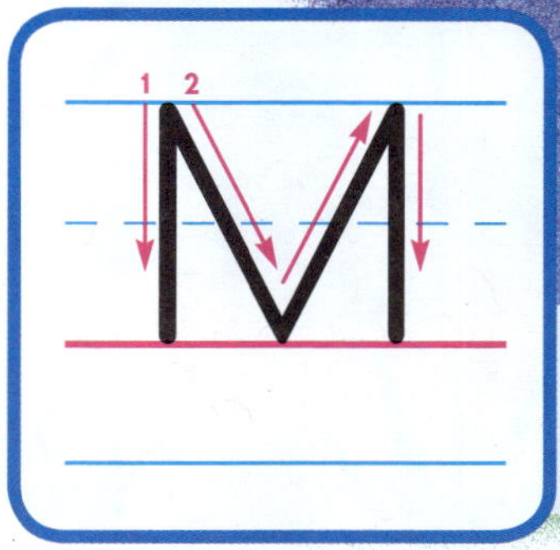

1. Pull down straight. Lift.
2. Slant right. Slant up. Pull down straight.

Trace and write. ✓ Circle your best **M**.

M M M M M M

Moo Megan Matt

Digital Tutor
Letter Model and Formation

Write

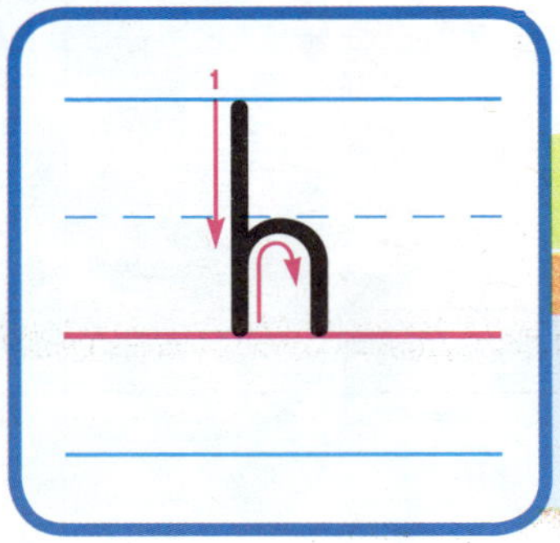

1. Pull down straight.
Push up; curve forward;
pull down straight.

Trace and write. Circle your best **h**.

h h h h h h h

hen hat hill

Digital Tutor
Letter Model and Formation

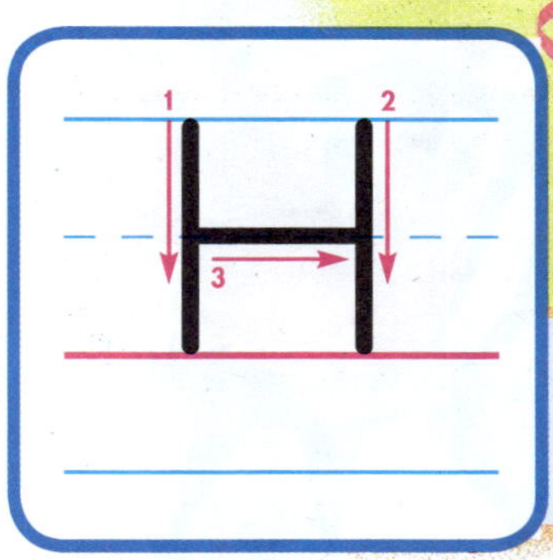

1. Pull down straight. Lift.
2. Pull down straight. Lift.
3. Slide right.

Trace and write. ✔ Circle your best **H**.

H H H H H H H

Helen Hen Happy

Digital Tutor
Letter Model and Formation

Review

Write the letters.

r r n n m m h h

R R N N M M H H

Lowercase Letters Write the missing lowercase letters.

k

v w x y z

Write

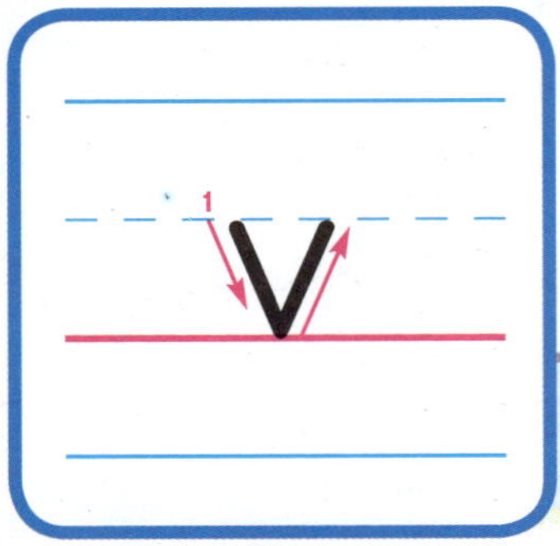

1. Slant right.
Slant up.

Trace and write. Circle your best **v**.

v v v v v v v

violin violets vase

Digital Tutor
Letter Model and Formation

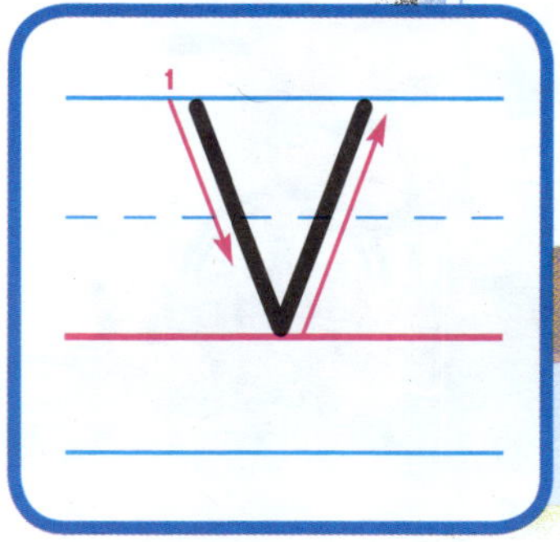

Trace and write. ✔ Circle your best **V**.

V V V V V V V

Van Vinny Val

Digital Tutor

Letter Model and Formation

Write

1. Slant right. Lift.
2. Slant left.

Trace and write. ✔ Circle your best **y**.

y y y y y y y

yo-yo yellow yarn

Digital Tutor
Letter Model and Formation

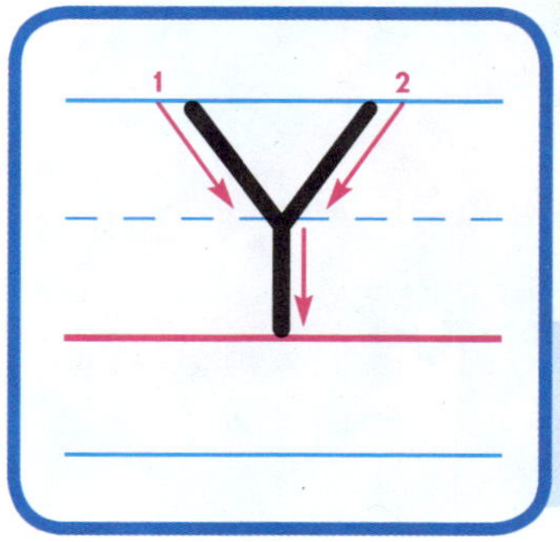

1. Slant right. Lift.
2. Slant left. Pull down straight.

Trace and write. ✓ Circle your best **Y**.

Y Y Y Y Y Y Y

Yard Yoko Yana

Digital Tutor

Letter Model and Formation

Write

1. Slant right. Slant up.
Slant right. Slant up.

Trace and write. Circle your best **w**.

w w w w w w w

wagon wheel window

Digital Tutor
Letter Model and Formation

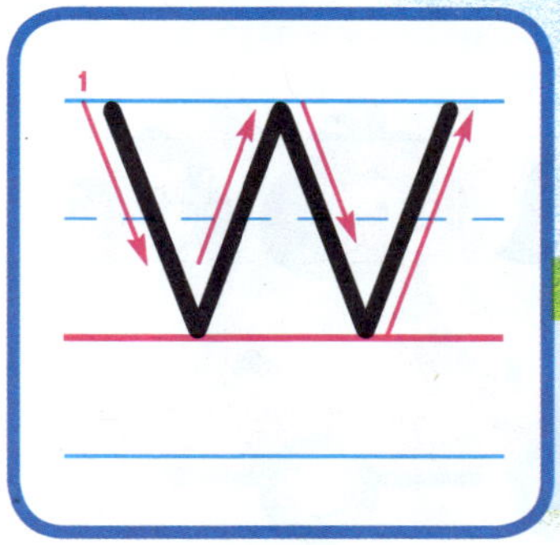

1. Slant right. Slant up.
Slant right. Slant up.

Trace and write. ✓ Circle your best **W**.

W W W W W W

Welcome Walt Will

Digital Tutor

Letter Model and Formation

Review

Write the letters.

v v

y y

w w

V V

Y Y

W W

Uppercase Letters Write the missing uppercase letters.

K

X Z

Write

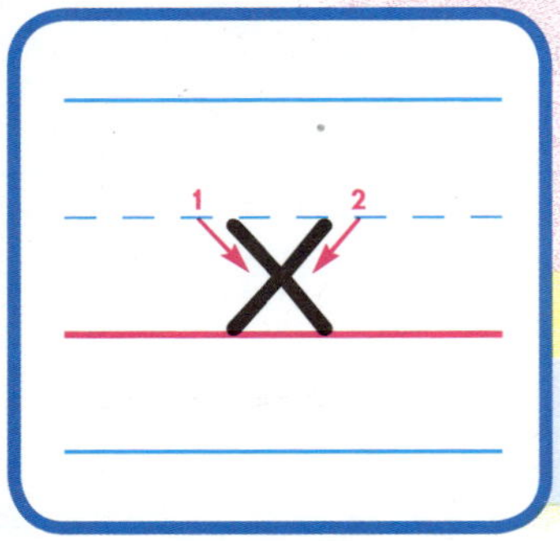

1. Slant right. Lift.
2. Slant left.

Trace and write. Circle your best **x**.

x x x x x x x

fox box ox

Digital Tutor

Letter Model and Formation

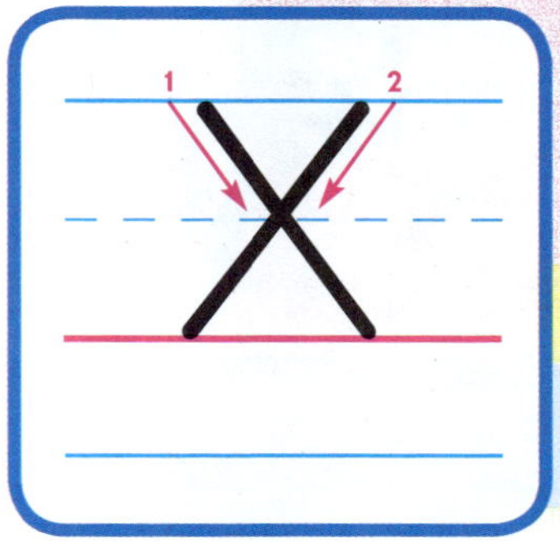

1. Slant right. Lift.
2. Slant left.

Trace and write. Circle your best **X**.

X X X X X X X

EXIT Xavier Xiang

Digital Tutor
Letter Model and Formation

Write

k

1. Pull down straight. Lift.
2. Slant left. Slant right.

Trace and write. ✔ Circle your best **k**.

k k k k k k k

kite key king

Digital Tutor
Letter Model and Formation

Write

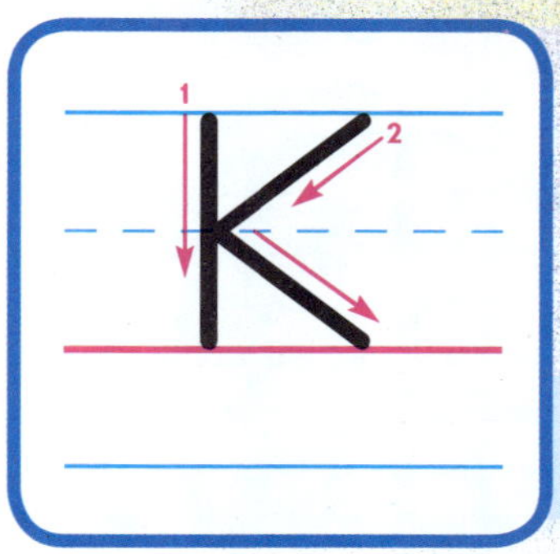

1. Pull down straight. Lift.
2. Slant left. Slant right.

Trace and write. ✓ Circle your best **K**.

K K K K K K K

Kittens Kate Kevin

Digital Tutor

Letter Model and Formation

Write

z

1. Slide right. Slant left. Slide right.

Trace and write. Circle your best **z**.

z z z z z z z

zebra zero zipper

Digital Tutor
Letter Model and Formation

1. Slide right. Slant left. Slide right.

Trace and write. Circle your best **Z**.

Z Z Z Z Z Z Z

Zoom Zoey Zack

Digital Tutor

Letter Model and Formation

Review

Write the letters.

x x

k k

z z

X X

K K

Z Z

Apply

Lowercase Letters Write the lowercase alphabet.

Apply

Uppercase Letters Write the uppercase alphabet.

Write

1. Dot.

Trace and write. ✔ Circle your best . .

Run. Pass. Kick.

Write

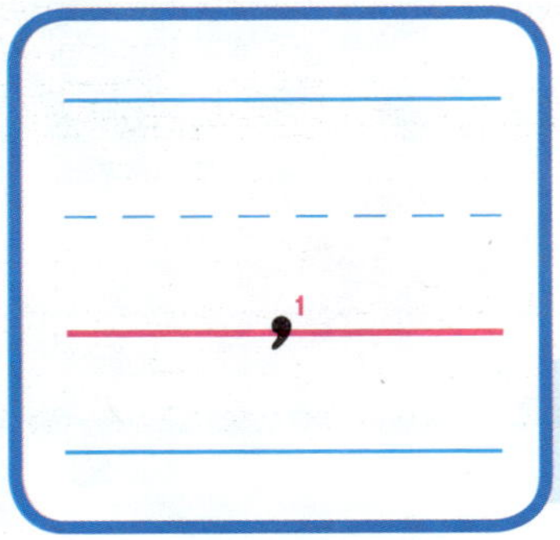

1. Dot; curve forward.

Trace and write. Circle your best , .

, , , , , , ,

a, b, c A, B, C

Write . and ,.

. . . . .

, , , , ,

Write the sentence.

Ready, set, go.

Write

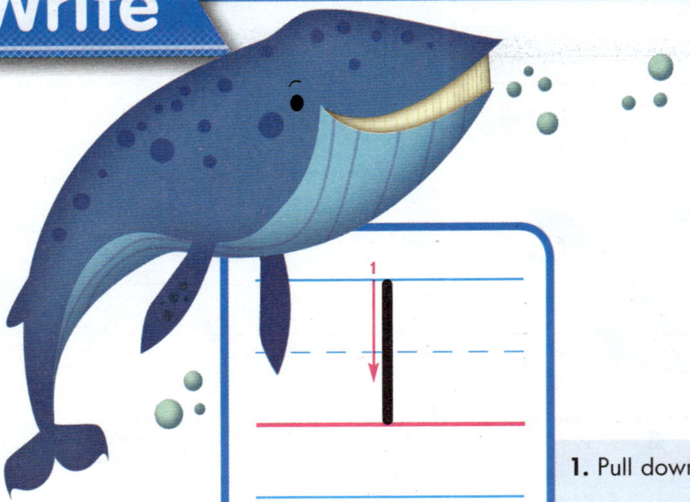

1

1. Pull down straight.

2

1. Curve forward; slant left. Slide right.

Trace and write. ✔ Circle your best **1** and your best **2**.

1 1 1 1

2 2 2 2

Digital Tutor

Numeral Models and Formations

3

1. Curve forward.
Curve forward.

4

1. Pull down straight.
Slide right. Lift.
2. Pull down straight.

Trace and write. ✔ Circle your best **3** and your best **4**.

3 3 3 3 4 4 4 4

Digital Tutor
Numeral Models and Formations

Write

1. Pull down straight. Circle forward. Lift.
2. Slide right.

1. Curve down; curve up and around.

Trace and write. ✔ Circle your best **5** and your best **6**.

5 5 5 5

6 6 6 6

Digital Tutor

Numeral Models and Formations

1. Slide right.
Slant left.

1. Curve back;
curve forward;
slant up.

Trace and write. Circle your best **7** and your best **8**.

7 7 7 7

8 8 8 8

Digital Tutor

Numeral Models and Formations

Write

1. Circle back all the way around. Pull down straight.

1. Pull down straight. Lift.
2. Curve down; curve up.

Trace and write. ✔ Circle your best **9** and your best **10**.

9 9 9 9

10 10 10

Digital Tutor

Numeral Models and Formations

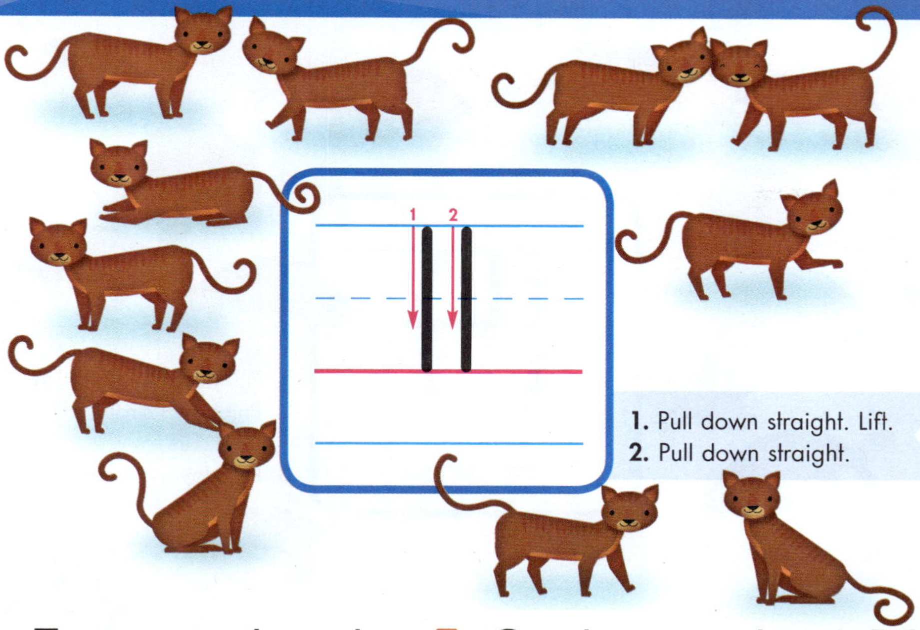

1. Pull down straight. Lift.
2. Pull down straight.

1. Pull down straight. Lift.
2. Curve forward; slant left. Slide right.

Trace and write. ✔ Circle your best **11** and your best **12**.

11 11 11 11

12 12 12 12

Digital Tutor

Numeral Models and Formations

Write

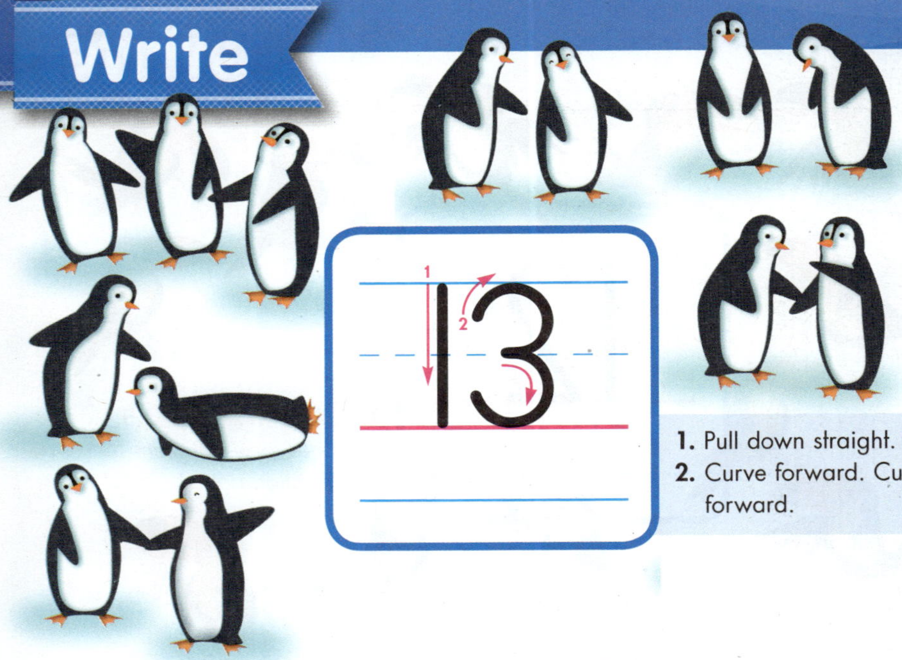

13

1. Pull down straight. Lift.
2. Curve forward. Curve forward.

14

1. Pull down straight. Lift.
2. Pull down straight. Slide right. Lift.
3. Pull down straight.

Trace and write. Circle your best **13** and your best **14**.

13 13 13 13

14 14 14 14

Digital Tutor

Numeral Models and Formations

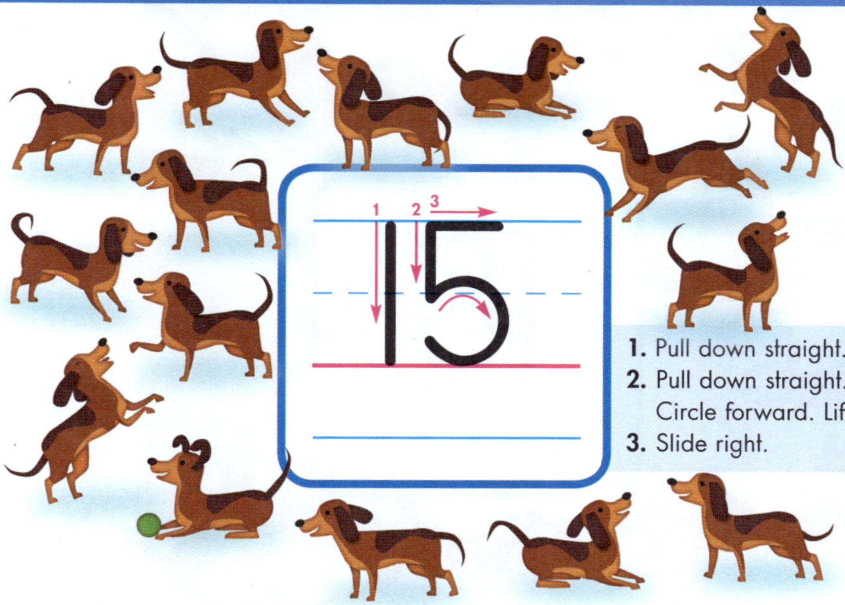

1. Pull down straight. Lift.
2. Pull down straight. Circle forward. Lift.
3. Slide right.

1. Pull down straight. Lift.
2. Curve down; curve up and around.

Trace and write. Circle your best **15** and your best **16**.

15 15 15 15

16 16 16 16

Digital Tutor

Numeral Models and Formations

Write

1. Pull down straight. Lift.
2. Slide right. Slant left.

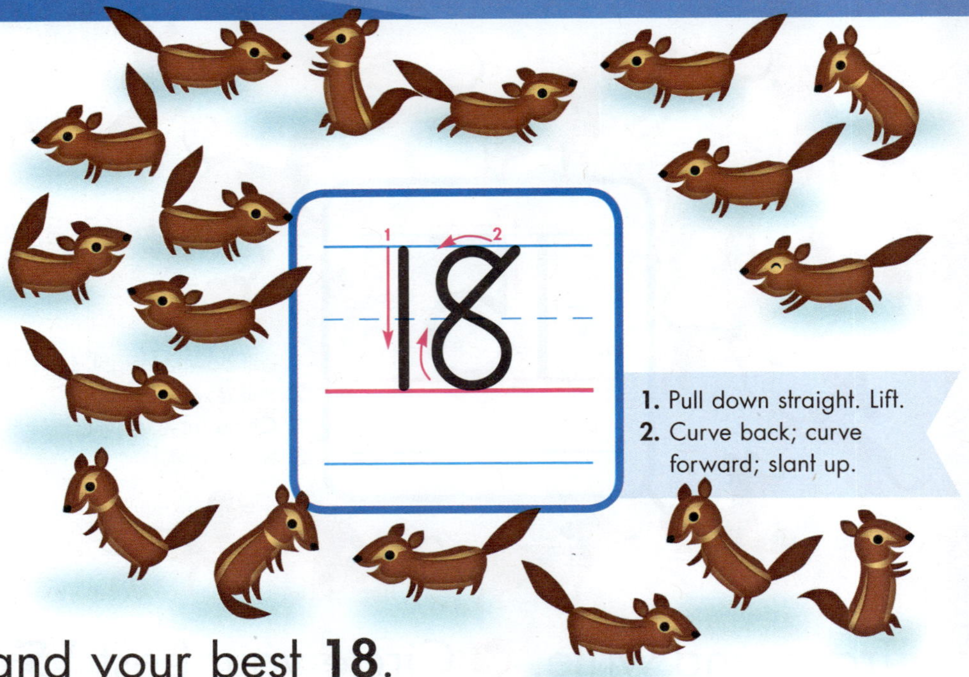

1. Pull down straight. Lift.
2. Curve back; curve forward; slant up.

Trace and write. Circle your best **17** and your best **18**.

17 17 17 17

18 18 18 18

Digital Tutor

Numeral Models and Formations

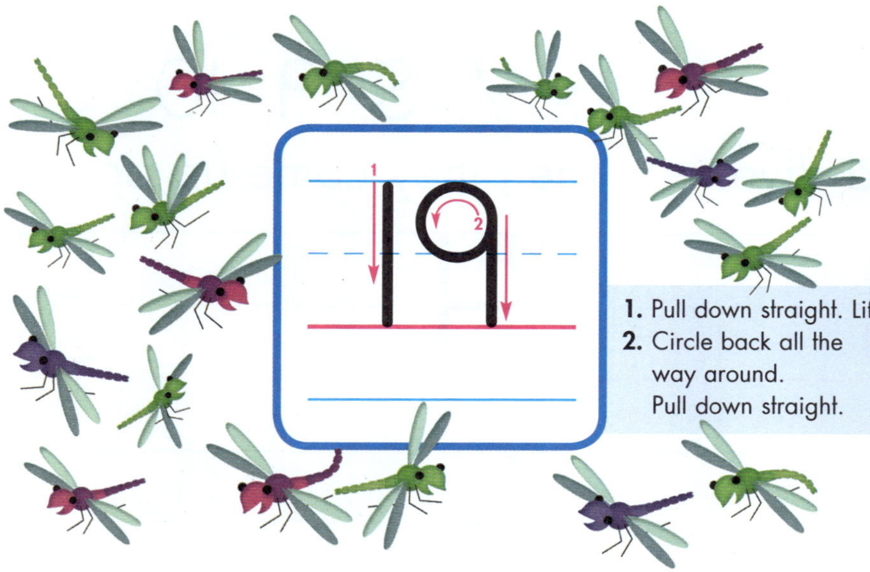

19

1. Pull down straight. Lift.
2. Circle back all the way around. Pull down straight.

20

1. Curve forward; slant left. Slide right. Lift.
2. Curve down; curve up.

Trace and write. Circle your best **19** and your best **20**.

19 19 19 19 20 20 20

Digital Tutor

Numeral Models and Formations

Review

Write the numbers.

1, 2, 3, 4, 5
Penguins jump and dive.

6, 7, 8, 9, 10
Then they come up again.

1 2 3 4 5

6 7 8 9 10

11, 12, 13, 14, 15
Birds stand and lean.

16, 17, 18, 19, 20
Then they fly away free.

11 12 13 14 15

16 17 18 19 20

Apply

Handwriting in the Real World

Number Words Write the numerals and the number words.

1 one

2 two

3 three

4 four

5 five

Write the numerals and the number words.

6 six

7 seven

8 eight

9 nine

10 ten

Apply

Handwriting in the Real World

Words Write the words.

dog

cat

sun

pig

Write the words.

ant

bee

cap

ball

Apply

Handwriting in the Real World

Sentences Write the sentences.

One dog plays piano.

Three dogs sing.

Apply

Write the sentences.

One bear cooks food.

Three bears eat.

Apply

Handwriting in the Real World

Note Write the note.

Dear Aunt Julia,

I miss you. Get well.

Love, Ethan

Informative/Explanatory

Invitation Write the invitation.

Come to our party.

It will be on Friday.

We will have fun.

Apply

Informative/Explanatory

Weather Report

Choose words to complete the sentences. Write the sentences.

warm

cold

sunny

rainy

Today is ______________.

It is ______________ outside.

Informative/Explanatory

The Weather Draw a picture about weather. Write words or sentences about your picture.

Apply

Informative/Explanatory

My Family Draw a picture of your family. Label each person or pet.

Apply

Write words or sentences about your family.

Apply

Narrative

My Super Power Pretend you have a super power. Draw a picture of yourself using your super power.

Apply

Write a short story about a time you used your super power. Include a beginning, a middle, and an ending.

Apply

Narrative

Story About My Friend Draw a picture of your friend. Write his or her name on the line.

Apply

Write a short story about something fun you did with your friend. Include a beginning, a middle, and an ending.

Apply

Opinion

My Favorite Book Draw a character or an event from your favorite book. Then write the title of your favorite book.

My favorite book is

Write one reason the book is your favorite.

Apply

Opinion

My Favorite Season Think about the four seasons. Circle your favorite season.

winter	spring	summer	fall

Draw a picture of your favorite season.

Write a sentence that tells why this season is your favorite.

Apply

Write What You Want! Draw a picture.

Apply

Write sentences about your picture.

Evaluate

Posttest

Write your name.

Write letters you know.

Write your address.

Credits

Art: Gail Armstrong: Cover; Kevin Zimmer: ii, 1, 5, 27; Bernard Adnet/Craven Design: iv, 10–11, 14–15, 18–19, 22–23, 28–29, 30–31, 101–103, 116–123, 139 (top); Kyle Poling/Liz Sanders Agency: 32–38, 40–46; Nathan Jarvis: 39, 47–63, 73, 83, 91, 99, 100; Tim Beaumont/Painted Words: 64–72, 74–82, 84–90, 92–98, 138, 139 (bottom); Nomar Perez/Painted Words: 104–115; Mircea Catusanu/Painted Words: 124

Photos: George C. Anderson Photography, Inc.: 6–7